National Park Explorers
YOSEMITE

by Sara Gilbert

CREATIVE EDUCATION · CREATIVE PAPERBACKS

TABLE OF CONTENTS

Some giant sequoia trees were made into tunnels.

WELCOME TO YOSEMITE NATIONAL PARK!

Look at those giant **granite** cliffs! Smell the pine trees. It smells like the wild here!

Yosemite is in California. It has
been a national park since 1890.

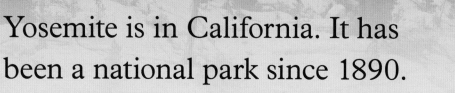

★ *Yosemite National Park*
■ *California*

Cathedral Peak and Upper Cathedral Lake (above); El Capitan and Merced River (right)

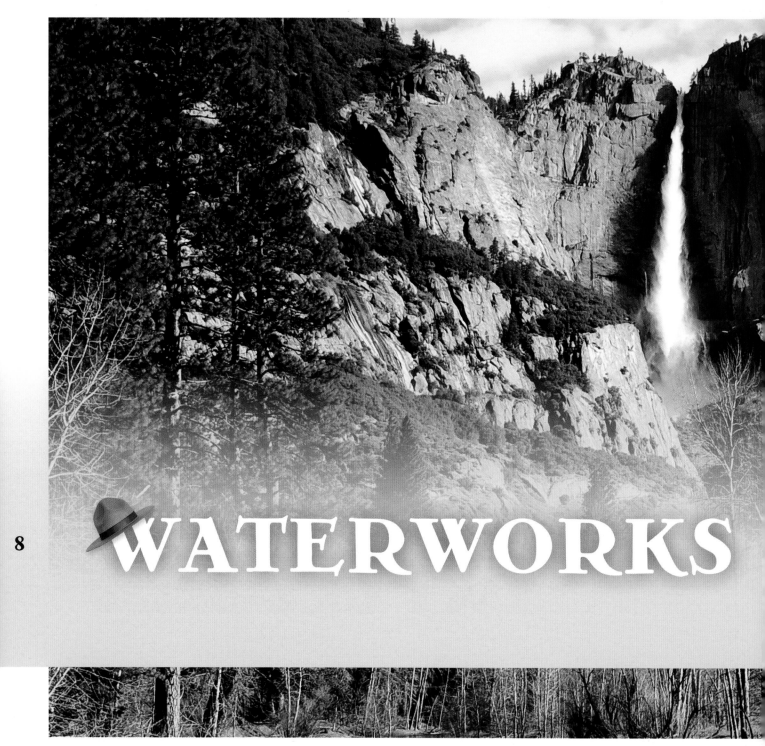

WATERWORKS

Yosemite is known for its **waterfalls**. Yosemite Falls drops 2,425 feet (739 m). It is one of the tallest waterfalls in the United States!

Water helped form Yosemite. Millions of years ago, **glaciers** wore down the rock. Now people climb the mountains.

Rock climbing at Lamb Dome (above); El Capitan (right)

LIFE IN THE PARK

Yosemite is home to many creatures. There are birds, bugs, black bears, and bobcats. Bighorn sheep climb the cliffs. Spotted owls hunt for small animals in the forests.

13

There are thousands of plants, too. The biggest are the giant **sequoia** (*sih-KWOY-uh*) trees. "Grizzly Giant" is a famous sequoia. It is about 1,800 years old! It stands 209 feet (63.7 m) tall.

Indian paintbrush (below); "Faithful Couple" giant sequoias (right)

CLIMBING AND CLASSES

ple visit Yosemite each year.
orseback riding, or rock
e an art class. Or you can go
s.

Rangers talk about the park's history. They show you how to take care of the park. They tell you how to stay safe around wild animals.

A deer (above); a Sierra mountain kingsnake (right)

Be sure to guard your food from bears in Yosemite. If you feed the animals, they won't be wild anymore. And Yosemite will always be a wild place!

Park visitors enjoy amazing wildlife and views.

Activity

WATCH A GLACIER MOVE

Materials needed:

1-pound box of
   cornstarch
Water
Large bowl
Spoon
Waxed paper
Gravel, sand, and soil

Step 1: Dump the cornstarch into a large bowl. Stir in 1½ cups water until just a little is still on the surface.

Step 2: Place a sheet of waxed paper on a flat surface. Spoon some of the cornstarch mixture onto the waxed paper. This will be your glacier.

Step 3: Sprinkle the sand, gravel, and soil on the waxed paper, leaving about an inch between it and the glacier.

Step 4: Add another spoonful of cornstarch mix to the glacier. What happens now? Does it move or stay put?

Step 5: Continue adding to the glacier. Write down how far it moves each time. What happens to the gravel, sand, and soil as it moves?

Glossary

glaciers — slow-moving masses of ice and snow

granite — a very hard rock often used in buildings

rangers — people who take care of a park

sequoia — a redwood tree that grows in California

waterfalls — places where water flows over a drop in a river or stream

Read More

McHugh, Erin. *National Parks: A Kid's Guide to America's Parks, Monuments, and Landmarks*. New York: Black Dog & Leventhal, 2012.

National Geographic. *National Geographic Kids National Parks Guide U.S.A.: The Most Amazing Sights, Scenes, and Cool Activities from Coast to Coast*. Washington, D.C.: National Geographic Society, 2012.

Websites

Kids Discover: National Parks
http://www.kidsdiscover.com/spotlight/national-parks-for-kids/
See pictures from the parks and learn more about their history.

WebRangers
http://www.nps.gov/webrangers/
Visit the National Park Service's site for kids to find fun activities.

Index

Published by Creative Education and Creative Paperbacks
P.O. Box 227, Mankato, Minnesota 56002 • Creative Education
and Creative Paperbacks are imprints of The Creative Company
www.thecreativecompany.us

Design and production by Christine Vanderbeek
Art direction by Rita Marshall
Printed in the United States of America

Photographs by Alamy (Brad Perks Lightscapes), Corbis (2/
Chris Hepburn/Ocean, Tracy Barbutes/Design Pics, NOAH
BERGER/epa, Cavan Images/Cavan Images, Jimmy Chin/
National Geographic Creative, Neale Clarke/Robert Harding
World Imagery, DK Limited, Ben Margot/AP, Tony Rowell, Jeff
Vanuga), Dreamstime (Belizar, Wisconsinart), Getty Images
(Kick Images), iStockphoto (MichaelSvoboda), Shutterstock
(Tarchyshnik Andrei, Don Fink, bogdan ionescu, Matt Jeppson,
Radoslaw Lecyk, Cosmin Manci, Paul B. Moore, Scenic
Shutterbug, Tomas Tichy, xpixel, Z.H.CHEN)

Library of Congress Cataloging-in-Publication Data
Gilbert, Sara. • Yosemite / by Sara Gilbert. • p. cm. —
(National park explorers) • *Summary*: A young explorer's
introduction to California's Yosemite National Park, covering
its mountain landscape, plants, animals such as black bears, and
activities such as rock climbing. • Includes index. • ISBN 978-
1-60818-635-8 (hardcover) • ISBN 978-1-62832-243-9 (pbk)
ISBN 978-1-56660-672-1 (eBook) • 1. Yosemite National Park
(Calif.)—Juvenile literature. I. Title.

F868.Y6G55 2016
979.4'47—dc23   2014048725

CCSS: RI.1.1, 2, 3, 4, 5, 6, 7, 10; RI.2.1, 2, 3, 5, 6, 7; RI.3.1, 3, 5,
7; RF.1.1, 3, 4; RF.2.4

First Edition HC 9 8 7 6 5 4 3 2 1
First Edition PBK 9 8 7 6 5 4 3 2 1